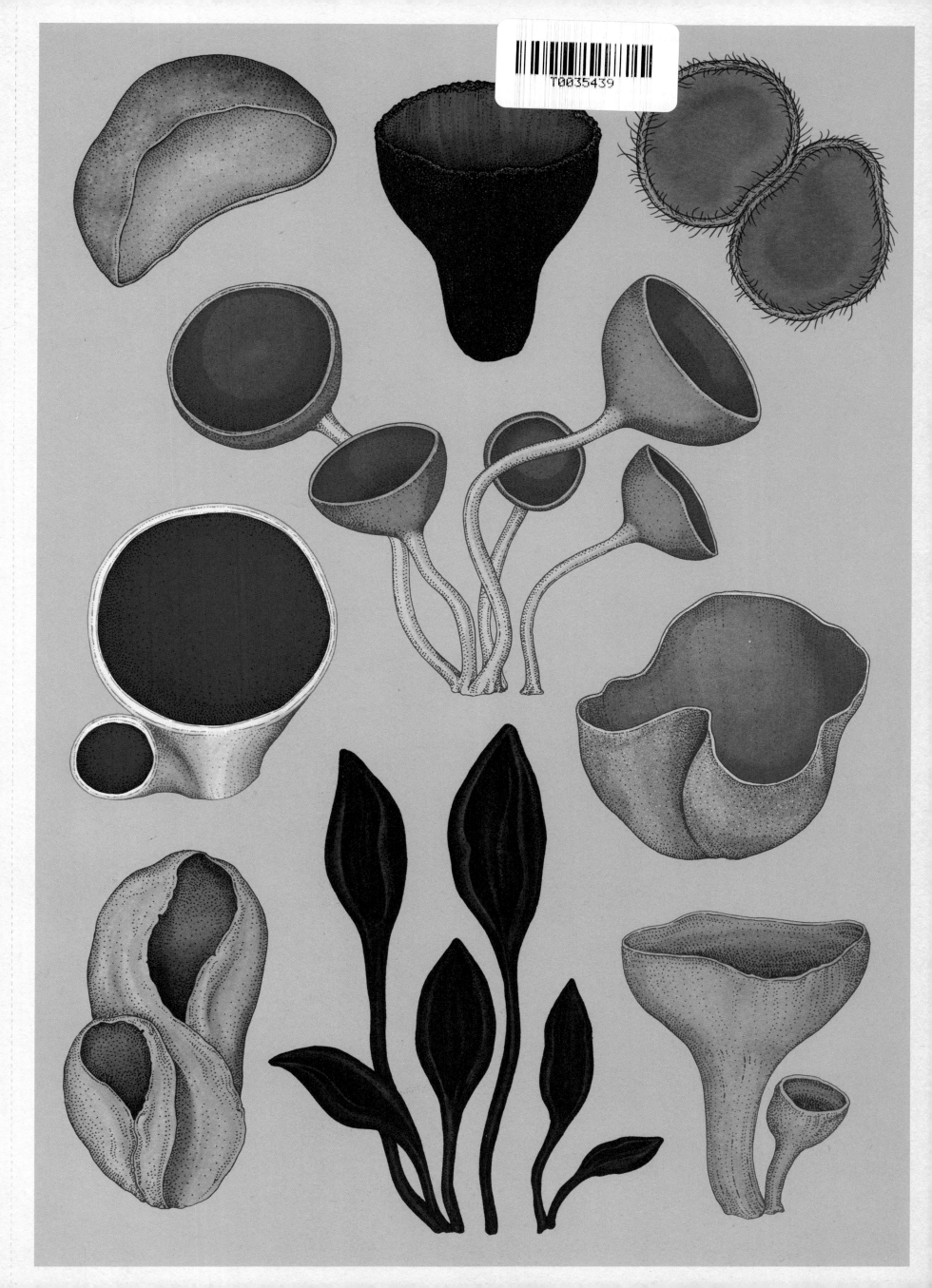

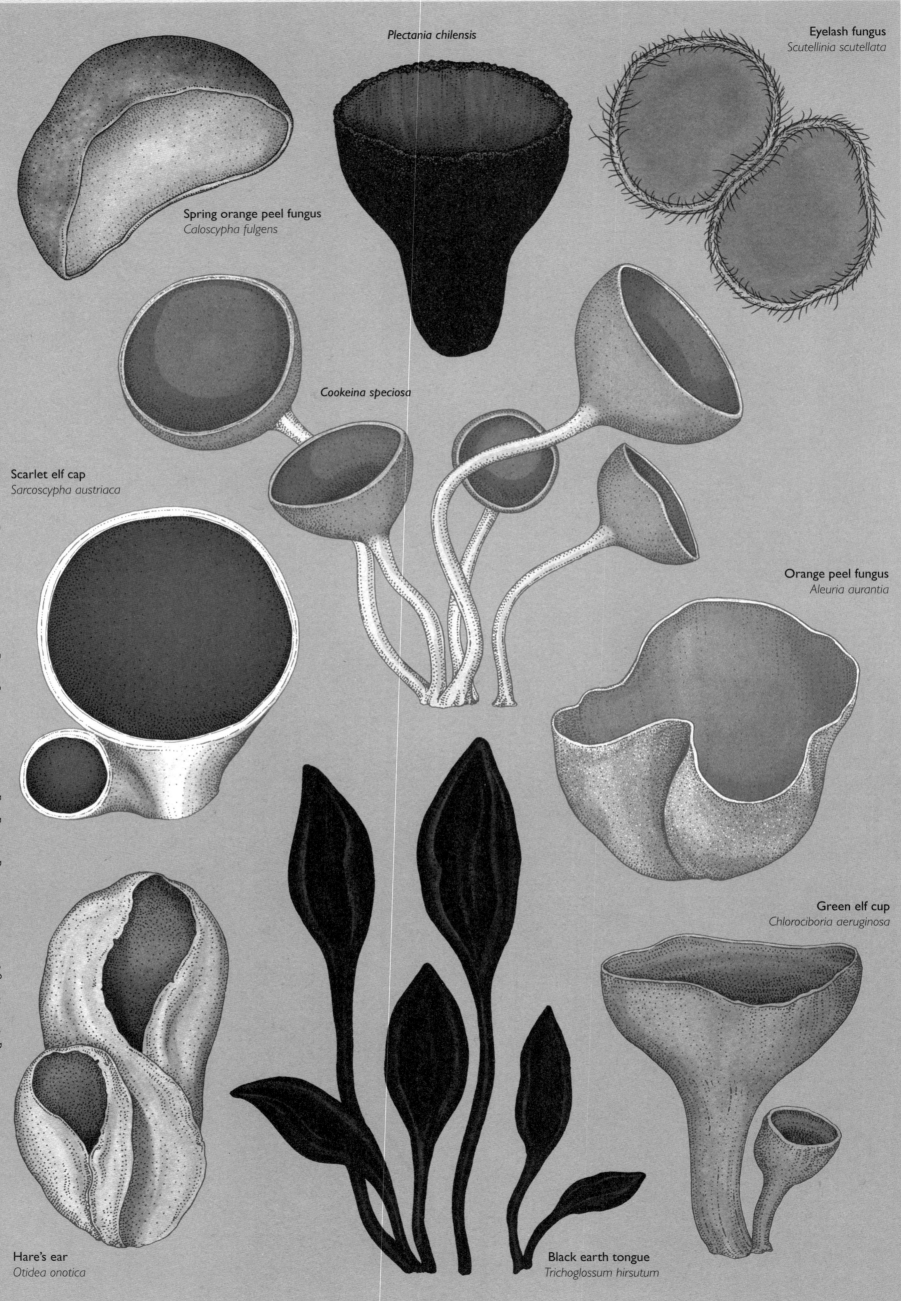

Spring orange peel fungus
Caloscypha fulgens

Plectania chilensis

Eyelash fungus
Scutellinia scutellata

Cookeina speciosa

Scarlet elf cap
Sarcoscypha austriaca

Orange peel fungus
Aleuria aurantia

Green elf cup
Chlorociboria aeruginosa

Hare's ear
Otidea onotica

Black earth tongue
Trichoglossum hirsutum

1: Alpine webcap
Cortinarius alpinus

2: Alpine brittlegill
Russula nana

3: Favre's fibercap
Inocybe favrei

4: Gassy webcap
Cortinarius traganus

5: Yellow stagshorn
Calocera viscosa

6: Stinking parachute
Gymnopus perforans

7: Weeping bolete
Suillus granulatus

8: Orange birch bolete
Leccinum versipelle

Shaggy ink cap
Coprinus comatus

Shaggy scalycap
Pholiota squarrosa

Waxcap
Hygrocybe sp.

Fly agaric
Amanita muscaria

Waxcap
Hygrocybe sp.

Blue roundhead
Stropharia caerulea

Waxcap
Hygrocybe sp.

Violet webcap
Cortinarius violaceus

Waxcap
Hygrocybe sp.

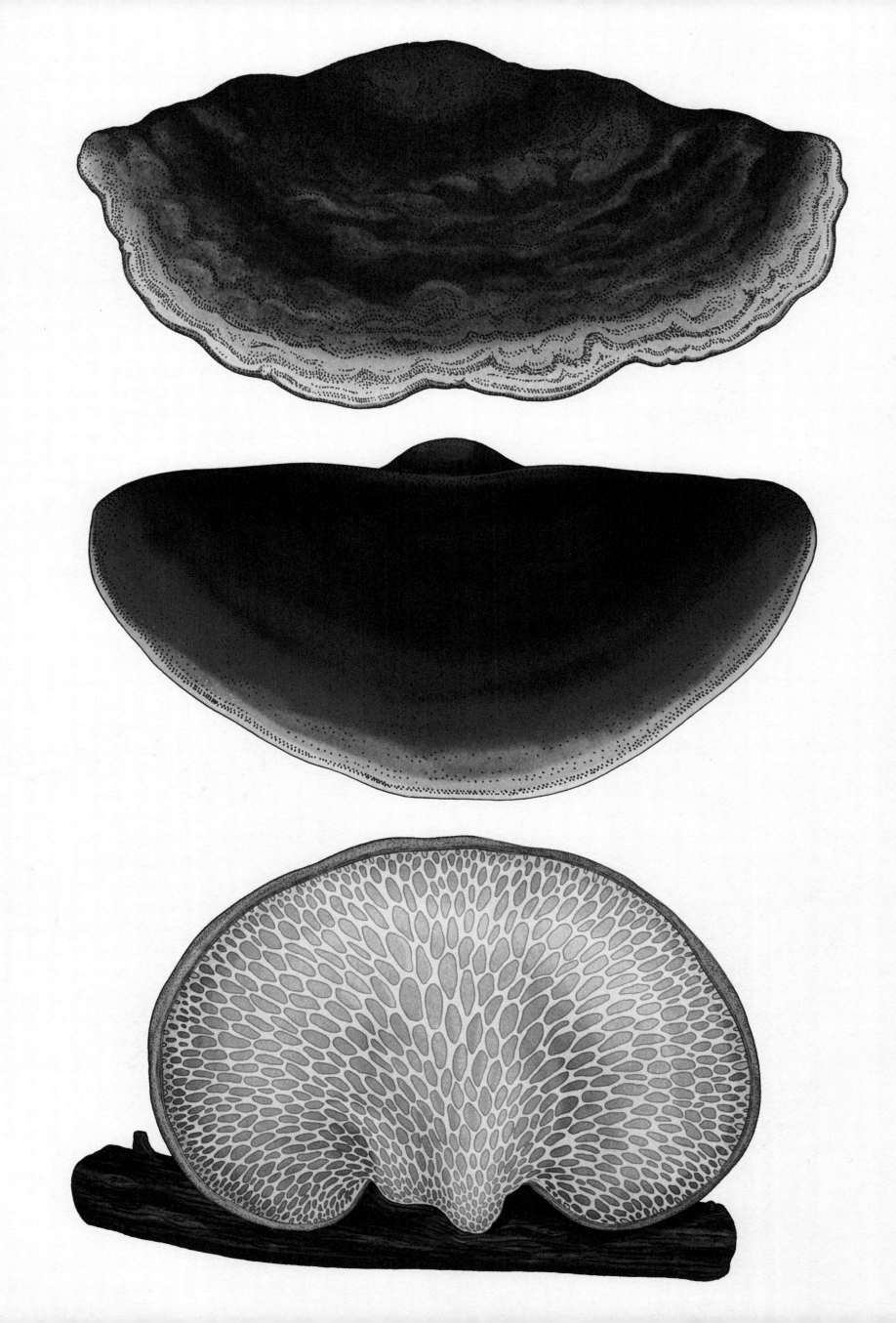

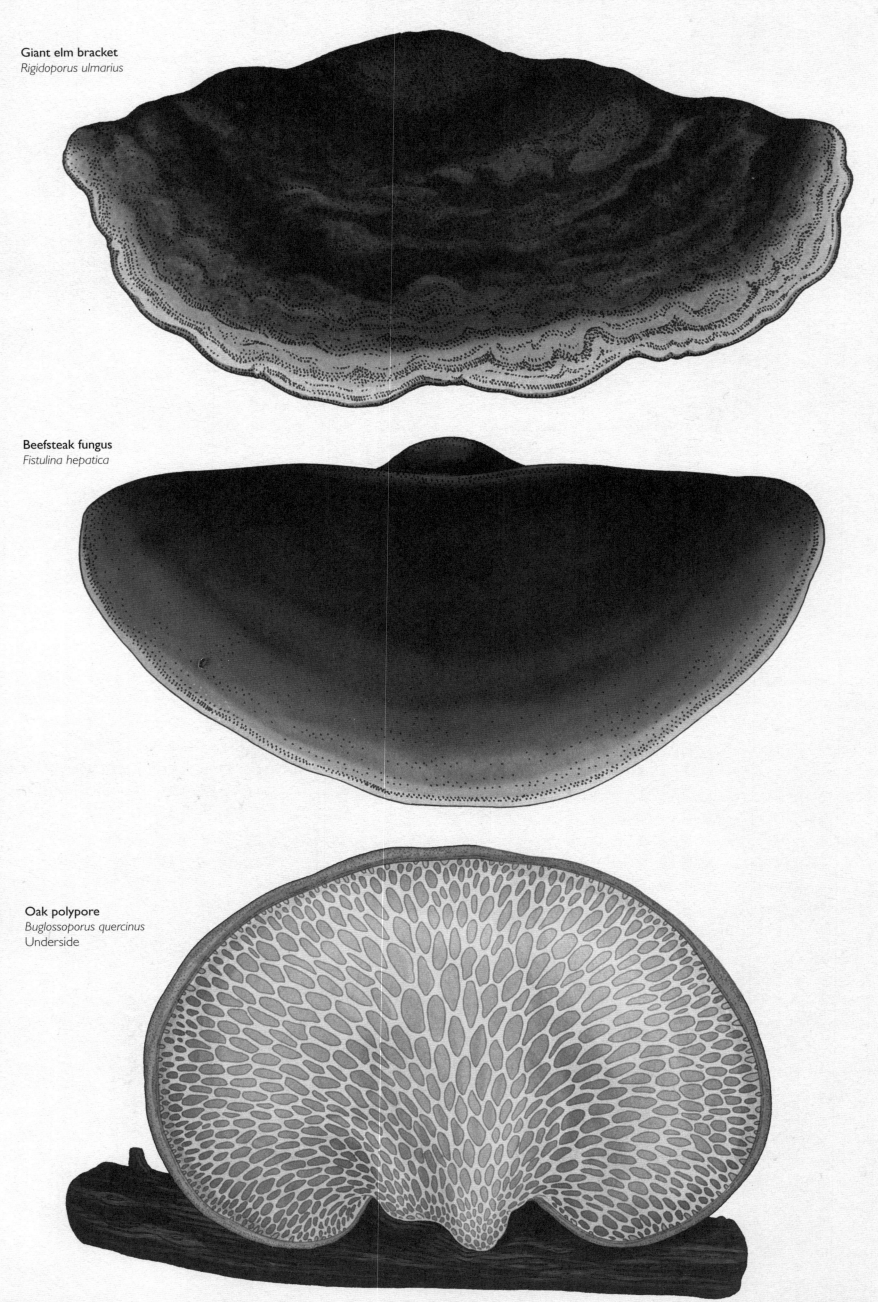

Giant elm bracket
Rigidoporus ulmarius

Beefsteak fungus
Fistulina hepatica

Oak polypore
Buglossoporus quercinus
Underside

Common puffball
Lycoperdon perlatum

Sculpted puffball
Calvatia sculpta

Bird's-nest fungus
Cyathus striatus

Stinkhorn fungus
Colus hirudinosus

Earthstar fungus
Geastrum quadrifidum

Rounded earthstar
Geastrum saccatum

Veiled lady
Phallus indusiatus

Common earthball
Scleroderma citrinum
Cross section

Common earthball
Scleroderma citrinum

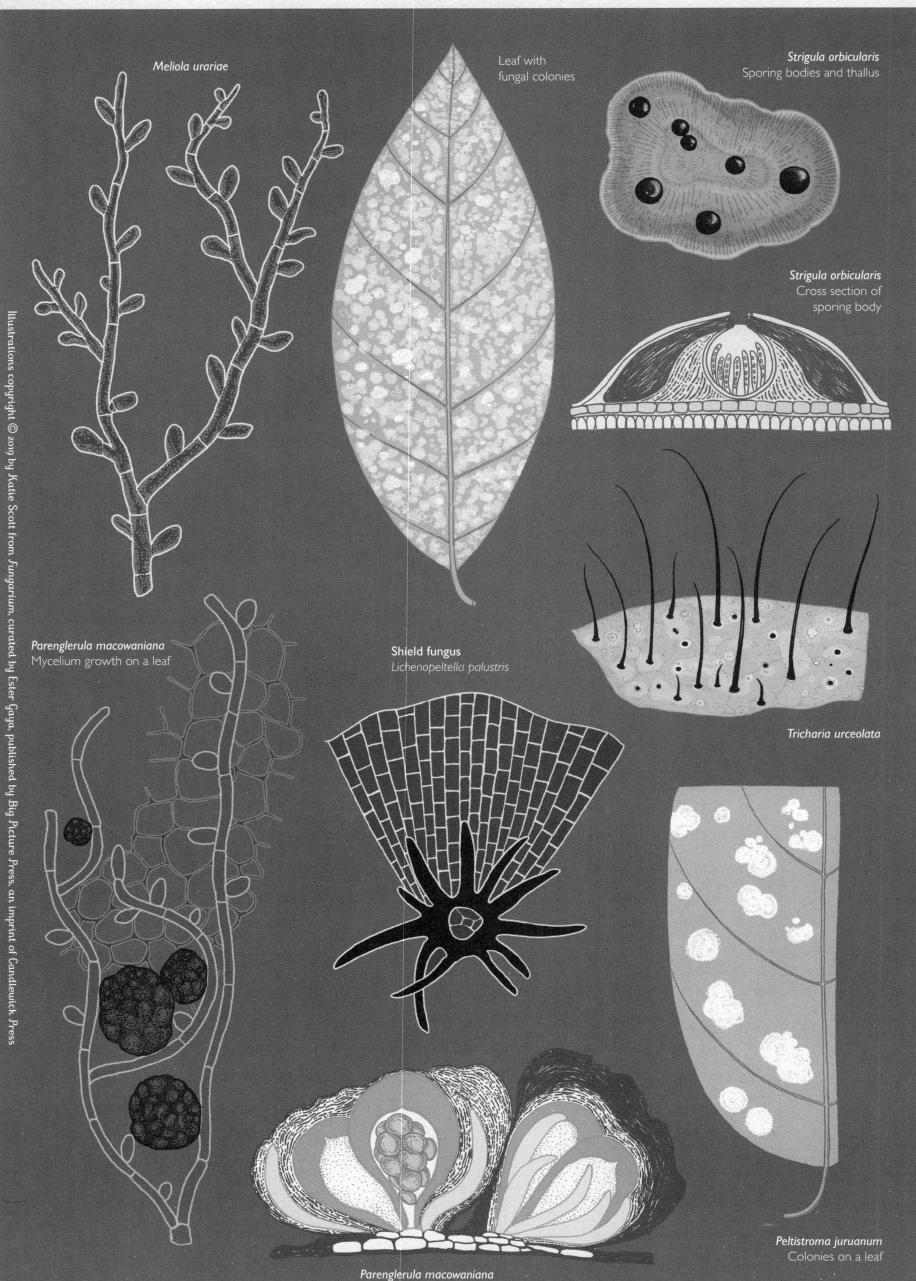

Meliola urariae

Leaf with
fungal colonies

Strigula orbicularis
Sporing bodies and thallus

Strigula orbicularis
Cross section of
sporing body

Parenglerula macowaniana
Mycelium growth on a leaf

Shield fungus
Lichenopeltella palustris

Tricharia urceolata

Parenglerula macowaniana
Cross section of sporing body on a leaf

Peltistroma juruanum
Colonies on a leaf

1: **Oakmoss lichen**
Evernia prunastri

2: **Chicken of the woods**
Laetiporus sulphureus

3: **Beefsteak fungus**
Fistulina hepatica

4: **Zoned rosette**
Podoscypha multizonata

5: **Spindle toughshank**
Gymnopus fusipes

6: **Oak milkcap**
Lactarius quietus

7: **Clustered bonnet**
Mycena inclinata

8: **Yellowfoot or
trumpet chanterelle**
Craterellus tubaeformis

9: **Coral fungi**
Ramaria sp.

10: **Beech or slimy milkcap**
Lactarius blennius

11: **Common earthball**
Scleroderma citrinum

12: **Matte bolete**
Xerocomellus pruinatus

13: **Tree lungwort lichen**
Lobaria pulmonaria

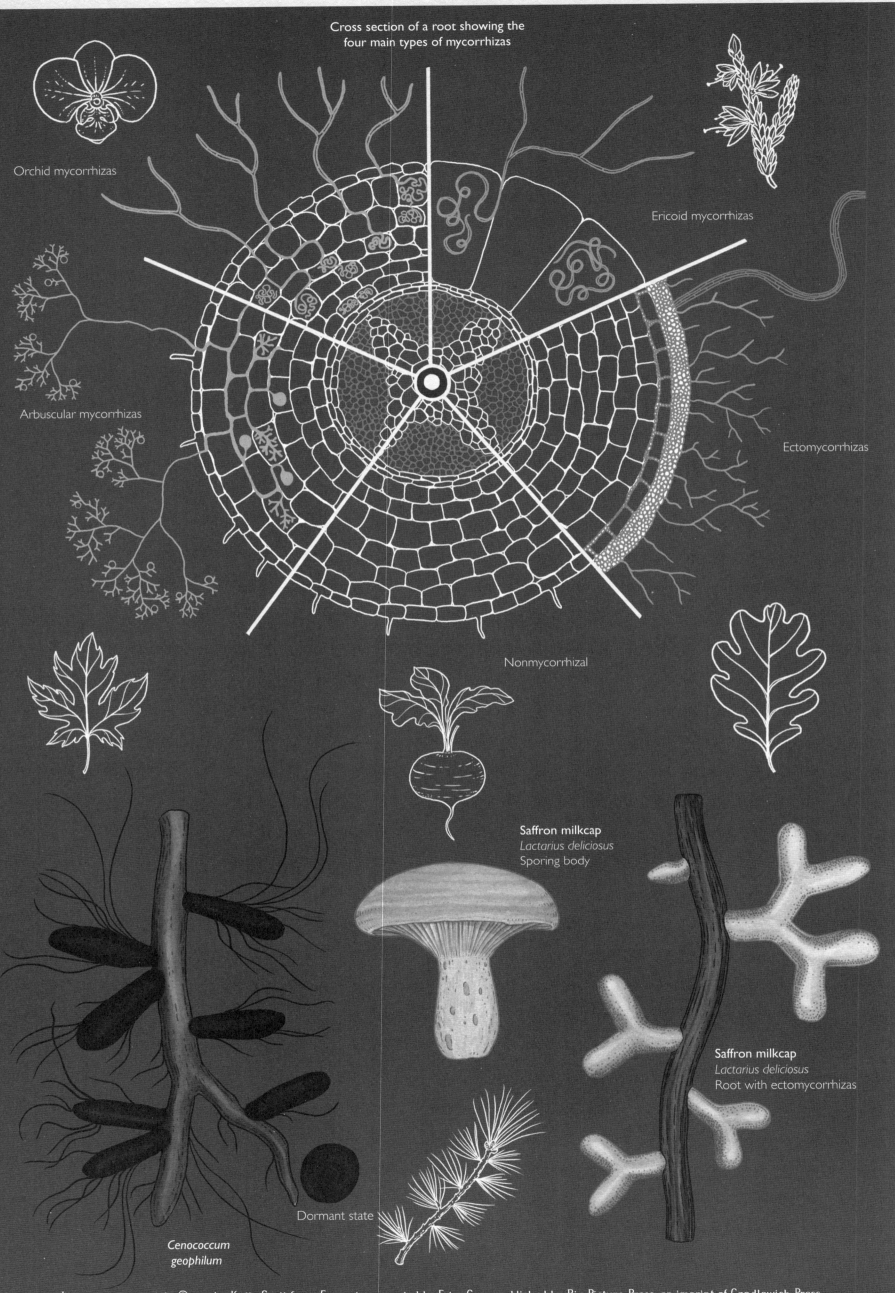

Cross section of a root showing the
four main types of mycorrhizas

Orchid mycorrhizas

Ericoid mycorrhizas

Arbuscular mycorrhizas

Ectomycorrhizas

Nonmycorrhizal

Saffron milkcap
Lactarius deliciosus
Sporing body

Saffron milkcap
Lactarius deliciosus
Root with ectomycorrhizas

*Cenococcum
geophilum*

Dormant state

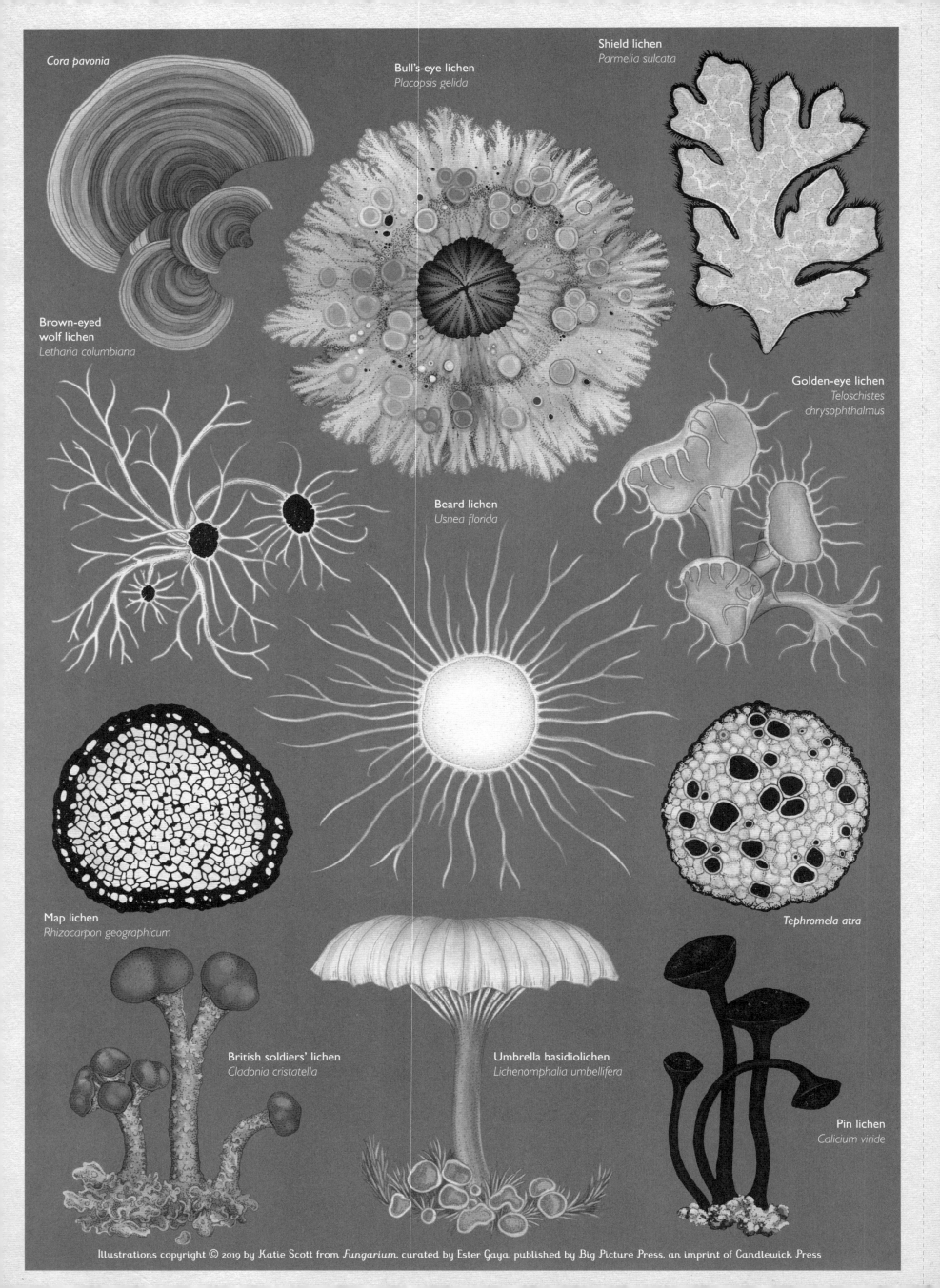

Cora pavonia

Bull's-eye lichen
Placopsis gelida

Shield lichen
Parmelia sulcata

Brown-eyed
wolf lichen
Letharia columbiana

Golden-eye lichen
Teloschistes chrysophthalmus

Beard lichen
Usnea florida

Map lichen
Rhizocarpon geographicum

Tephromela atra

British soldiers' lichen
Cladonia cristatella

Umbrella basidiolichen
Lichenomphalia umbellifera

Pin lichen
Calicium viride

Dong chong xia cao
Ophiocordyceps sinensis

Wasp fungus
Ophiocordyceps humbertii

Weevil fungus
Ophiocordyceps curculionum

Ant fungus
Pandora formicae

Zombie ant fungus
Ophiocordyceps unilateralis

Caterpillar fungus
Cordyceps militaris

White muscardine disease
Beauveria bassiana

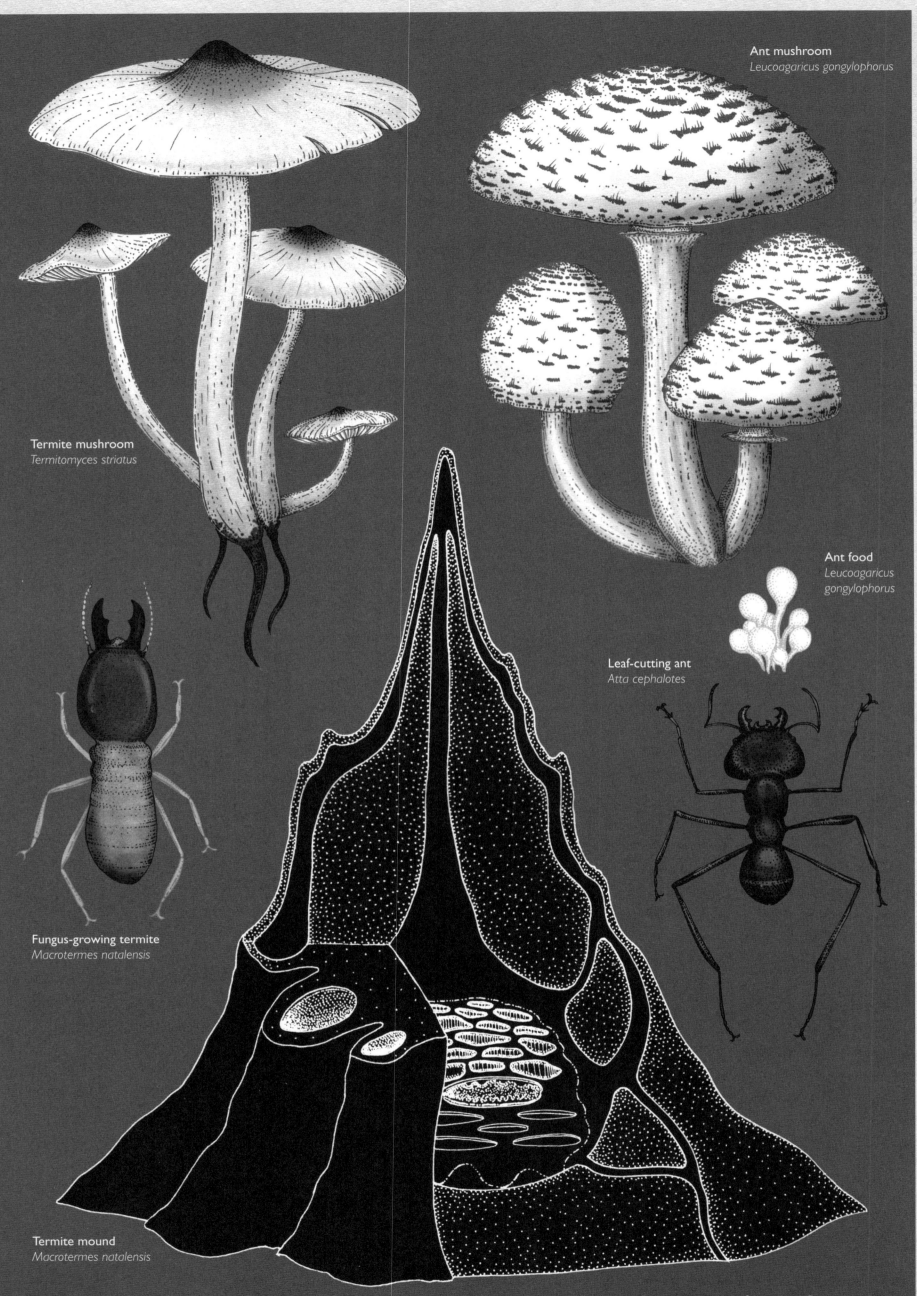

Ant mushroom
Leucoagaricus gongylophorus

Termite mushroom
Termitomyces striatus

Ant food
*Leucoagaricus
gongylophorus*

Leaf-cutting ant
Atta cephalotes

Fungus-growing termite
Macrotermes natalensis

Termite mound
Macrotermes natalensis

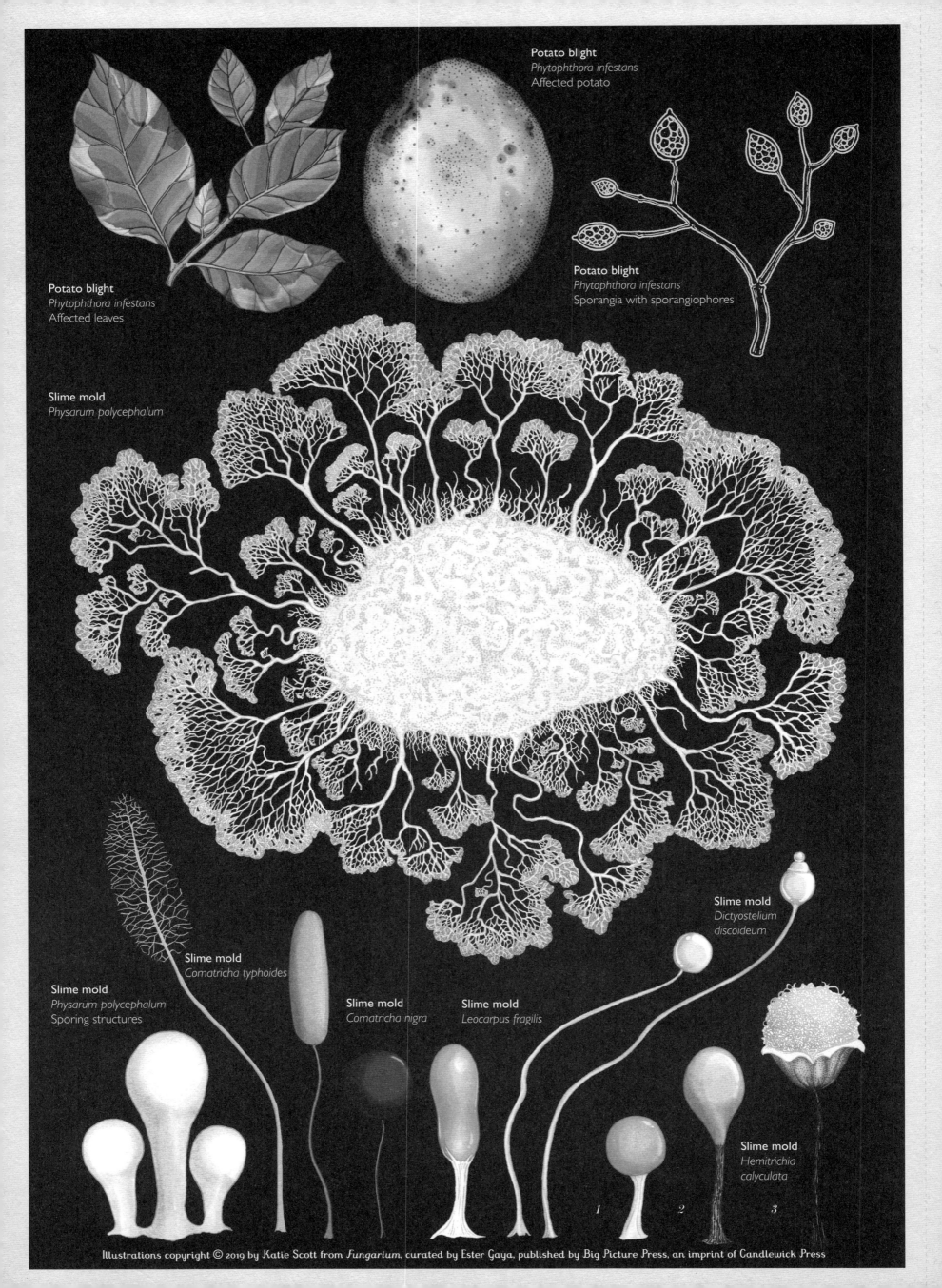

Potato blight
Phytophthora infestans
Affected leaves

Potato blight
Phytophthora infestans
Affected potato

Potato blight
Phytophthora infestans
Sporangia with sporangiophores

Slime mold
Physarum polycephalum

Slime mold
Physarum polycephalum
Sporing structures

Slime mold
Comatricha typhoides

Slime mold
Comatricha nigra

Slime mold
Leocarpus fragilis

Slime mold
Dictyostelium discoideum

Slime mold
Hemitrichia calyculata

1

2

3

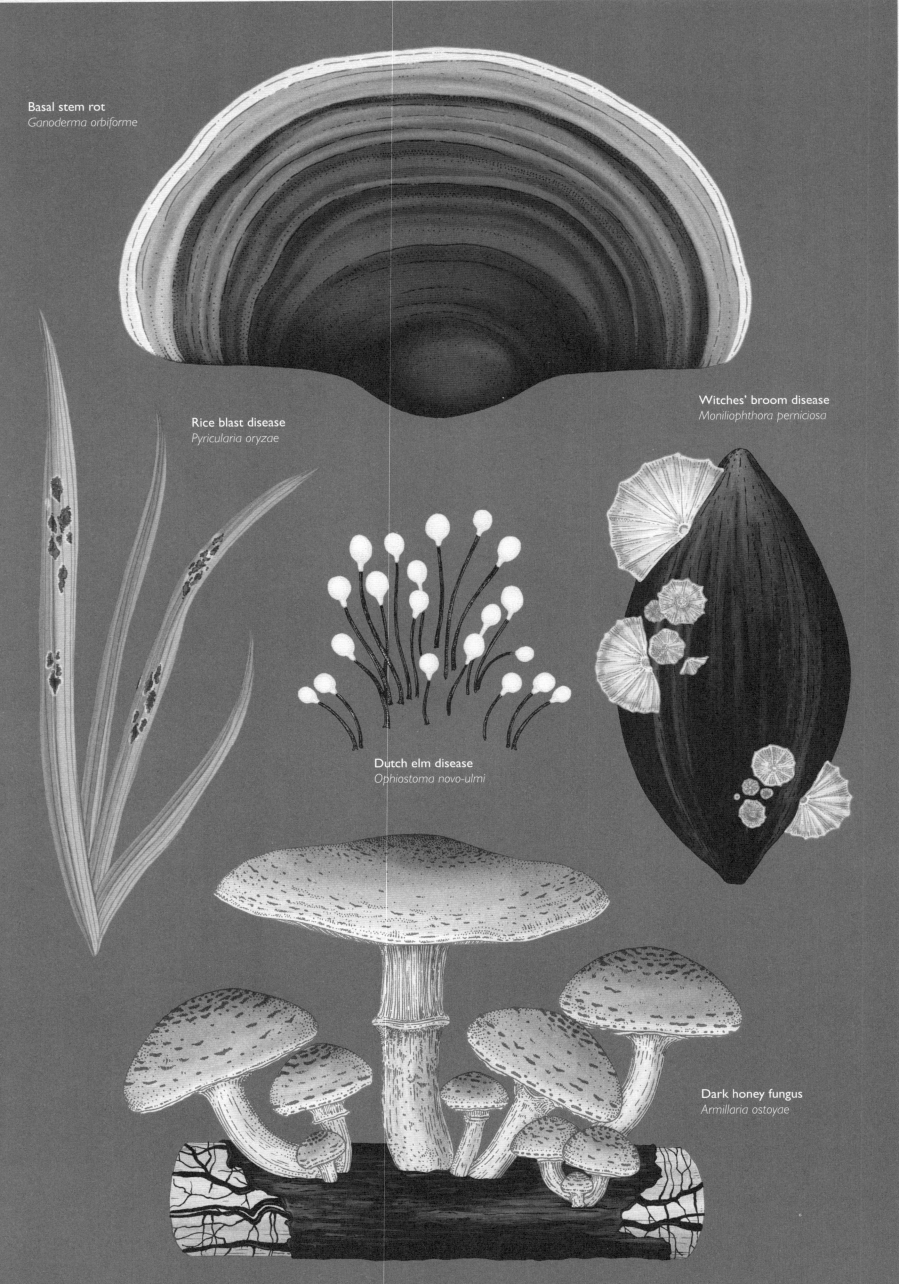

Basal stem rot
Ganoderma orbiforme

Rice blast disease
Pyricularia oryzae

Witches' broom disease
Moniliophthora perniciosa

Dutch elm disease
Ophiostoma novo-ulmi

Dark honey fungus
Armillaria ostoyae

Satan's bolete
Rubroboletus satanas

Satan's bolete
Rubroboletus satanas
Cross section

Kaentake
Trichoderma cornu-damae

Ergot fungus
Claviceps purpurea
On rye plant

Ergot fungus
Claviceps purpurea
Close-up of sporing bodies

Destroying angel
Amanita virosa

Death cap
Amanita phalloides

False morel
Gyromitra esculenta

Satan's bolete
Rubroboletus satanas

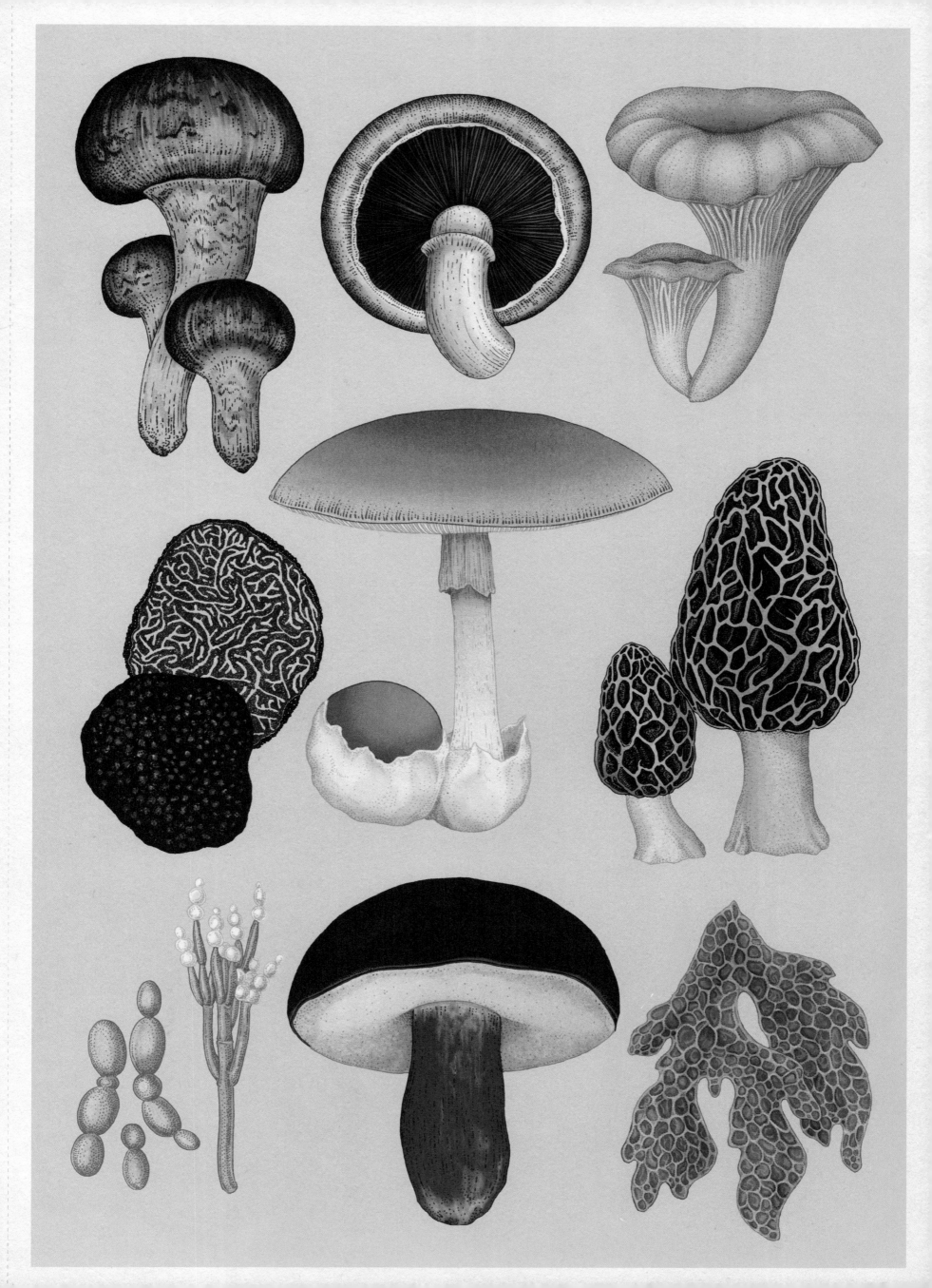

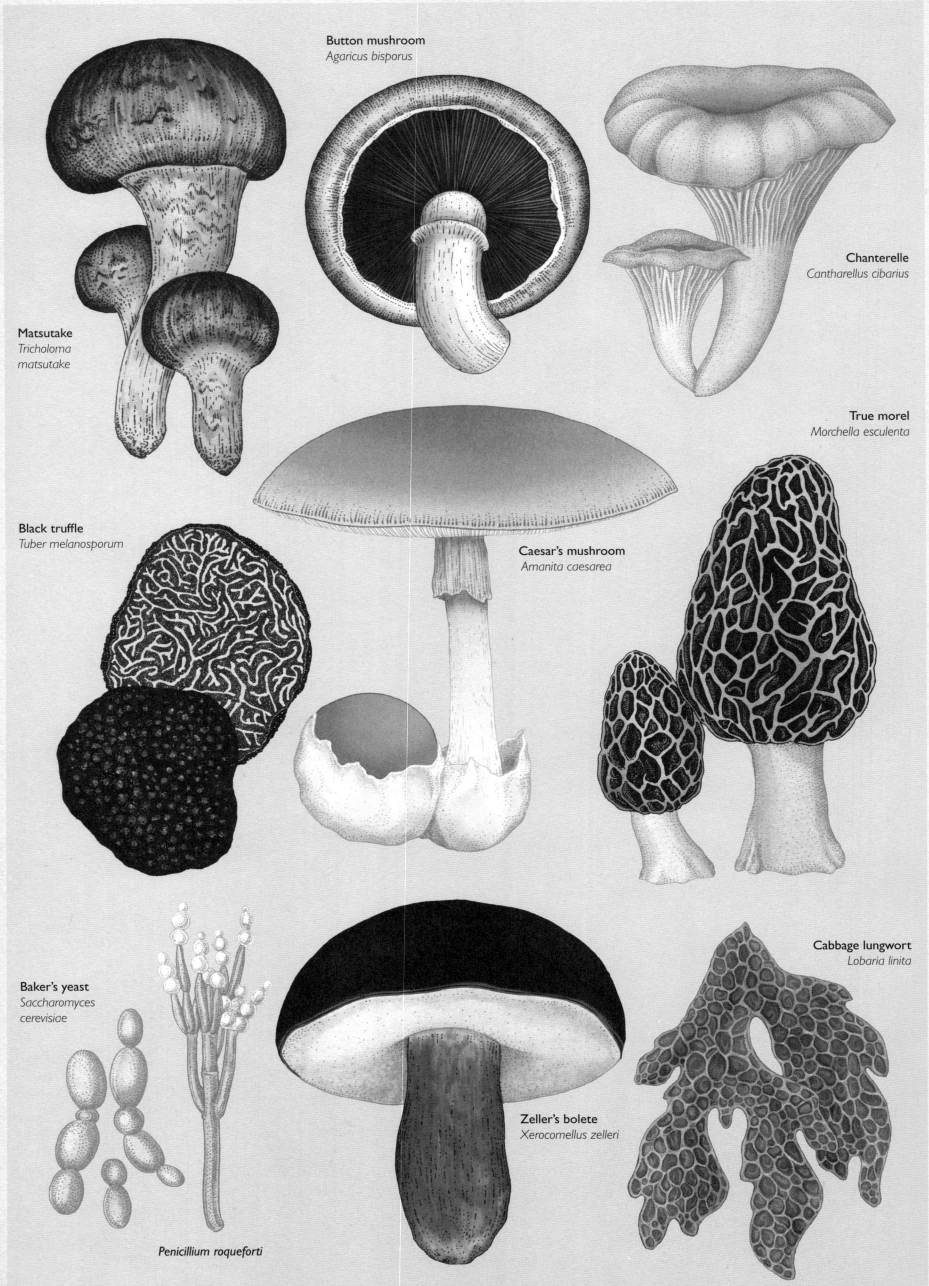

Button mushroom
Agaricus bisporus

Chanterelle
Cantharellus cibarius

Matsutake
Tricholoma matsutake

True morel
Morchella esculenta

Black truffle
Tuber melanosporum

Caesar's mushroom
Amanita caesarea

Cabbage lungwort
Lobaria linita

Baker's yeast
Saccharomyces cerevisiae

Penicillium roqueforti

Zeller's bolete
Xerocomellus zelleri

Glarea lozoyensis
Colony growing on a culture plate

Penicillium rubens
Colonies growing on a culture plate

Aspergillus terreus
Appearance under
a light microscope

Penicillium rubens
Appearance under
a light microscope

Isaria sinclairii
Infected cicada nymph

Aspergillus terreus
Colony growing on a culture plate

Tolypocladium inflatum
Colonies growing on a culture plate

1: Pleurotus djamor

2: Letrouitia domingensis

3: Deflexula subsimplex

4: Christmas wreath lichen
Herpothallon rubrocinctum

5: Spotted cort
Cortinarius iodes

6: Amethyst deceiver
Laccaria amethystina

7: Indigo milkcap
Lactarius indigo

8: Golden-scruffy collybia
Cyptotrama asprata

9: Cobalt crust
Terana coerulea

10: Pycnoporus sanguineus

11: Pod parachute
Gymnopus montagnei

12: Cookeina speciosa

13: Lactocollybia aurantiaca

14: Marasmius
haematocephalus

15: Parrot waxcap
Gliophorus psittacinus

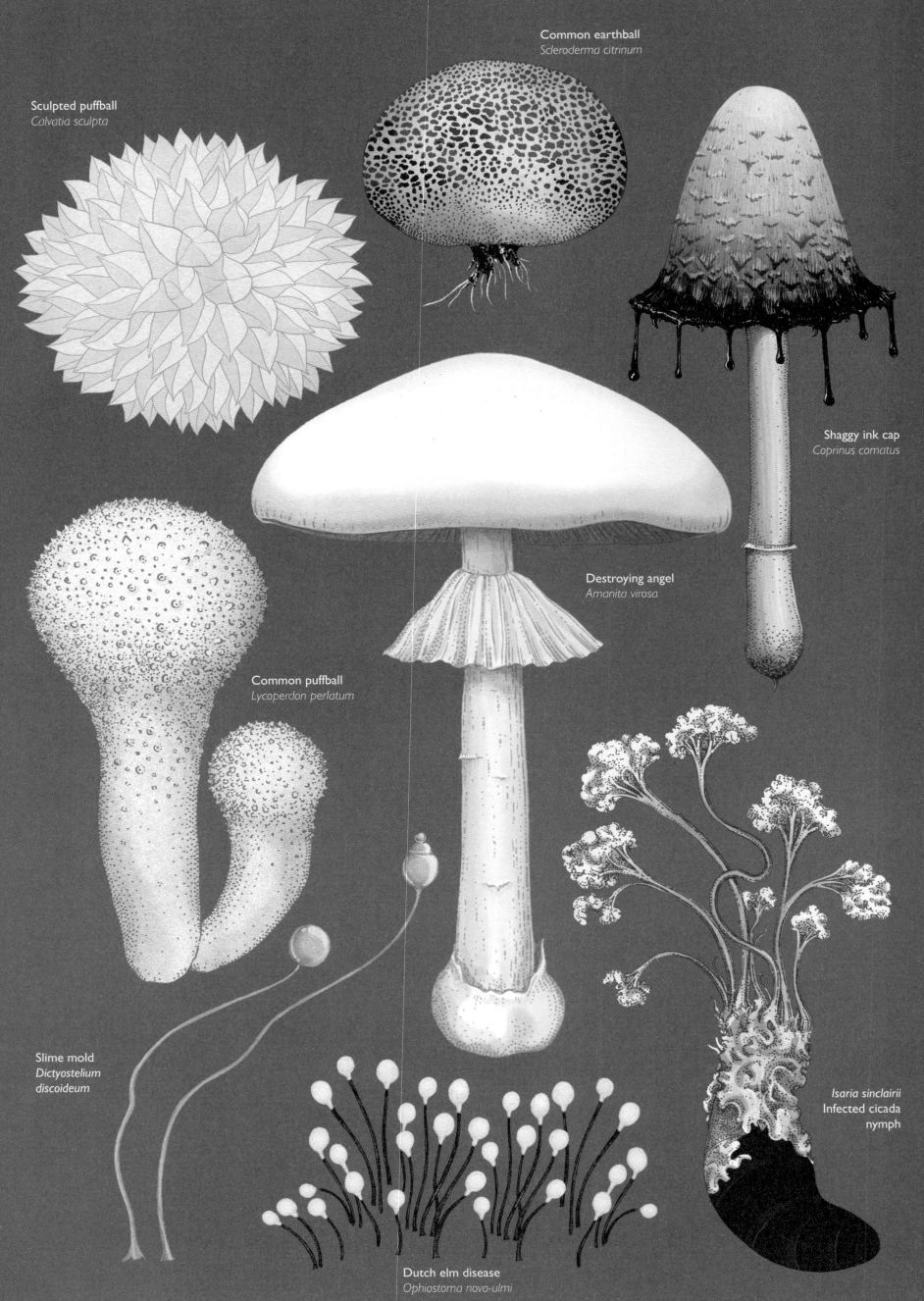

Sculpted puffball
Calvatia sculpta

Common earthball
Scleroderma citrinum

Shaggy ink cap
Coprinus comatus

Destroying angel
Amanita virosa

Common puffball
Lycoperdon perlatum

Slime mold
Dictyostelium discoideum

Isaria sinclairii
Infected cicada nymph

Dutch elm disease
Ophiostoma novo-ulmi

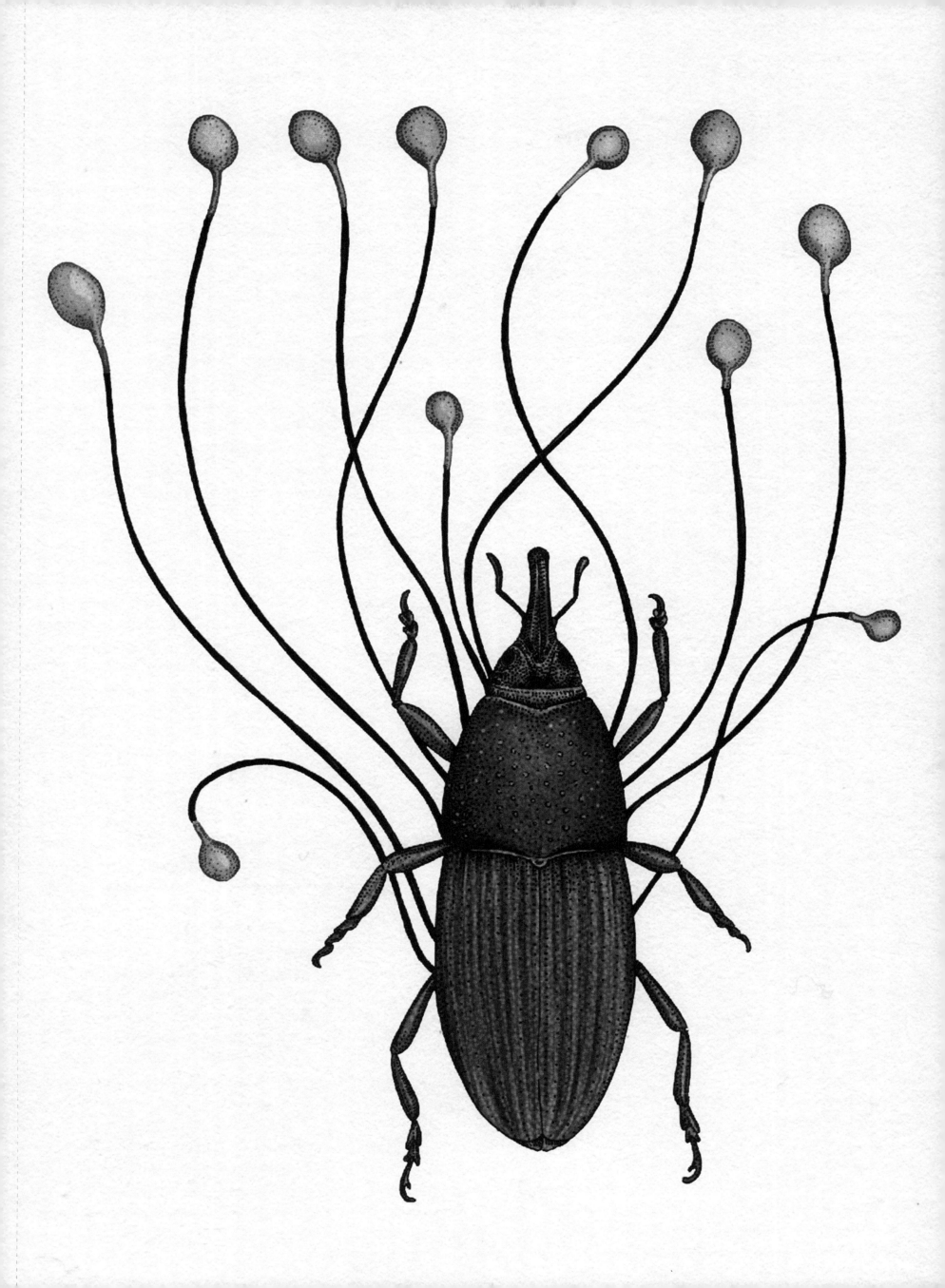

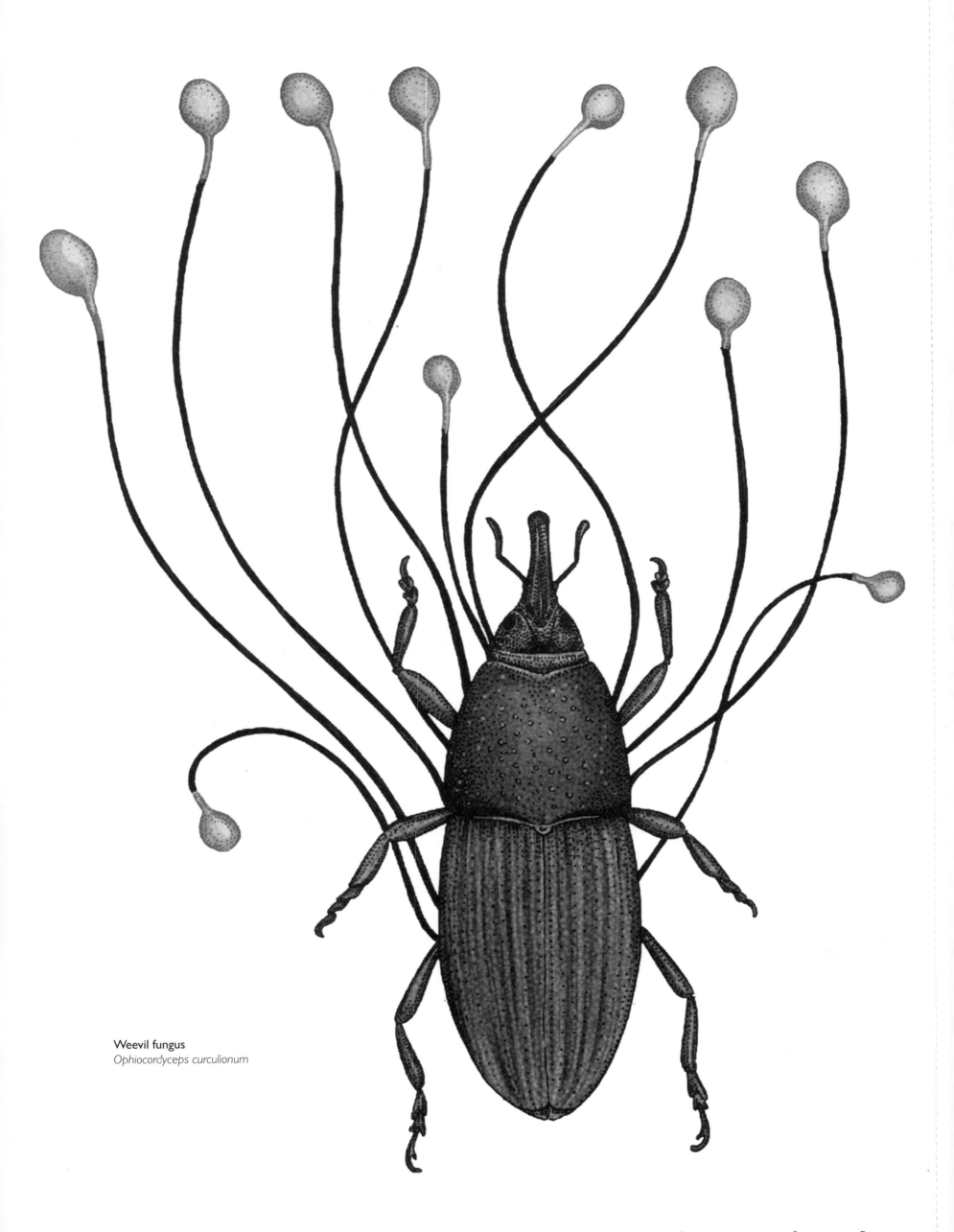

Weevil fungus
Ophiocordyceps curculionum

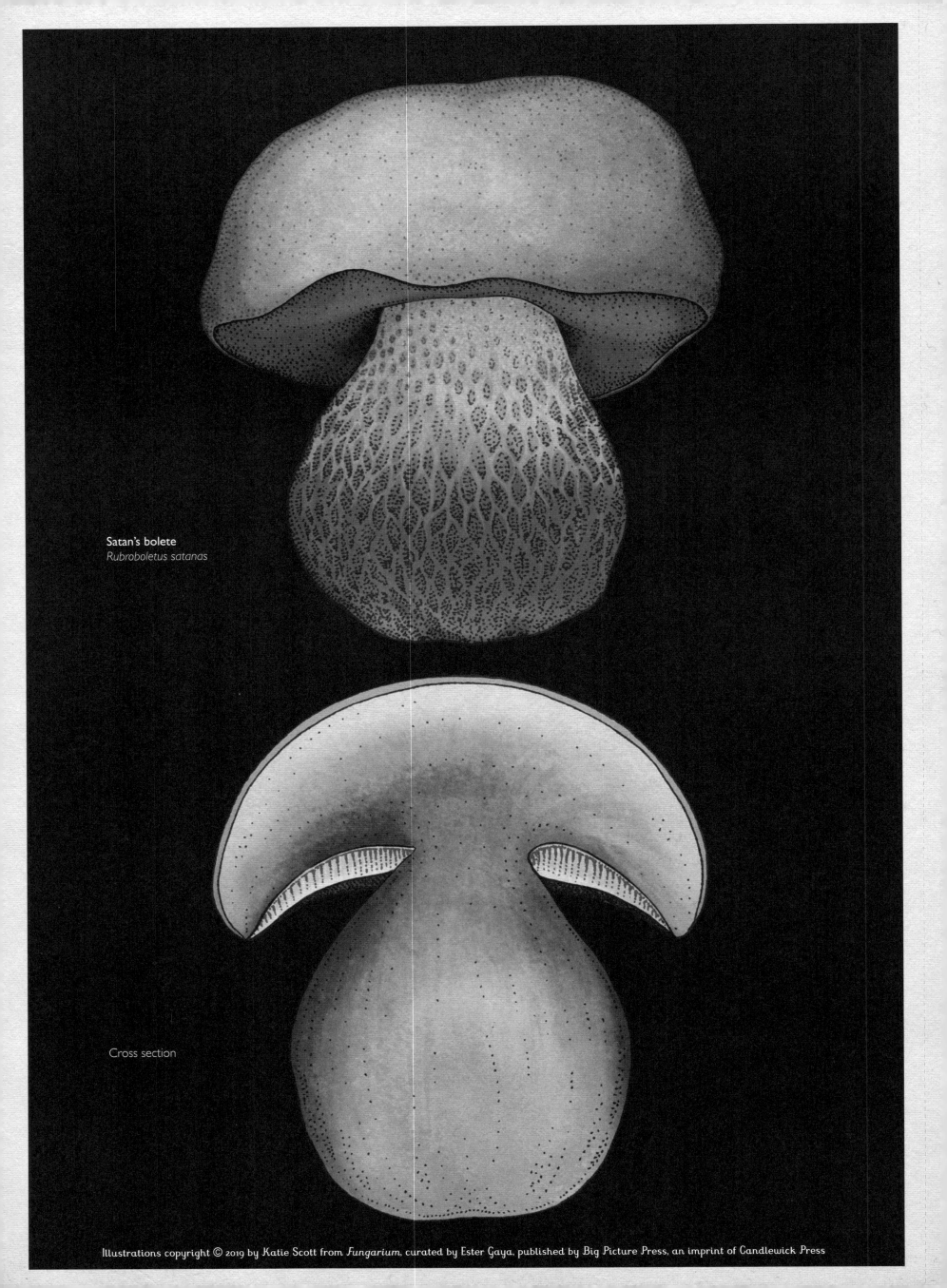

Satan's bolete
Rubroboletus satanas

Cross section

Fly agaric
Amanita muscaria

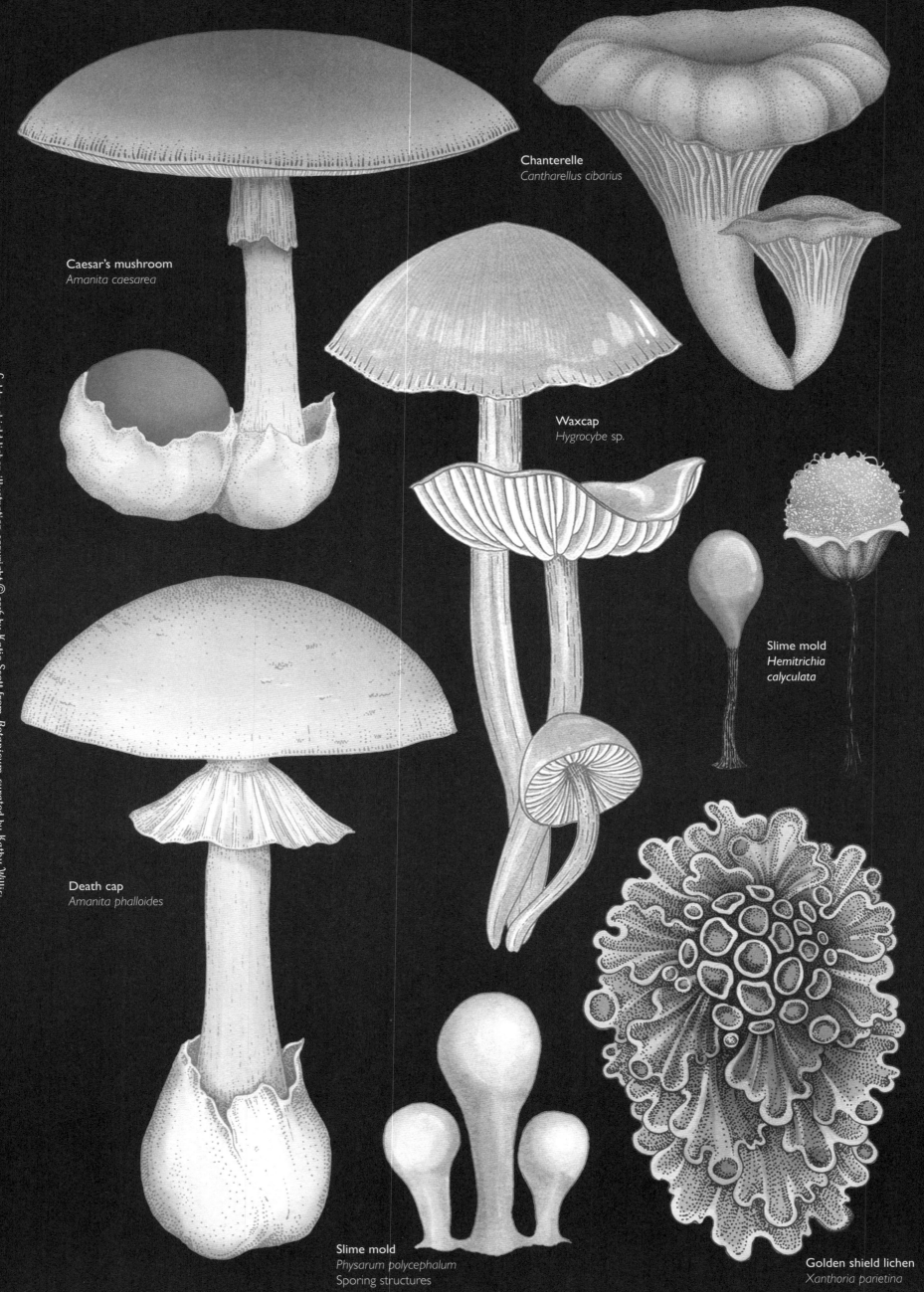

Caesar's mushroom
Amanita caesarea

Chanterelle
Cantharellus cibarius

Waxcap
Hygrocybe sp.

Slime mold
Hemitrichia calyculata

Death cap
Amanita phalloides

Slime mold
Physarum polycephalum
Sporing structures

Golden shield lichen
Xanthoria parietina

Turkey tail
Trametes versicolor

Violet webcap
Cortinarius violaceus

Blue roundhead
Stropharia caerulea

Cross section of satan's bolete
Rubroboletus satanas

Earthstar fungus
Geastrum quadrifidum

Leathery goblet
Cymatoderma elegans

Fly agaric
Amanita muscaria

Lane Cove waxcap
Hygrocybe lanecovensis

Waxcap
Hygrocybe sp.

Cookeina speciosa

Orange peel fungus
Aleuria aurantia

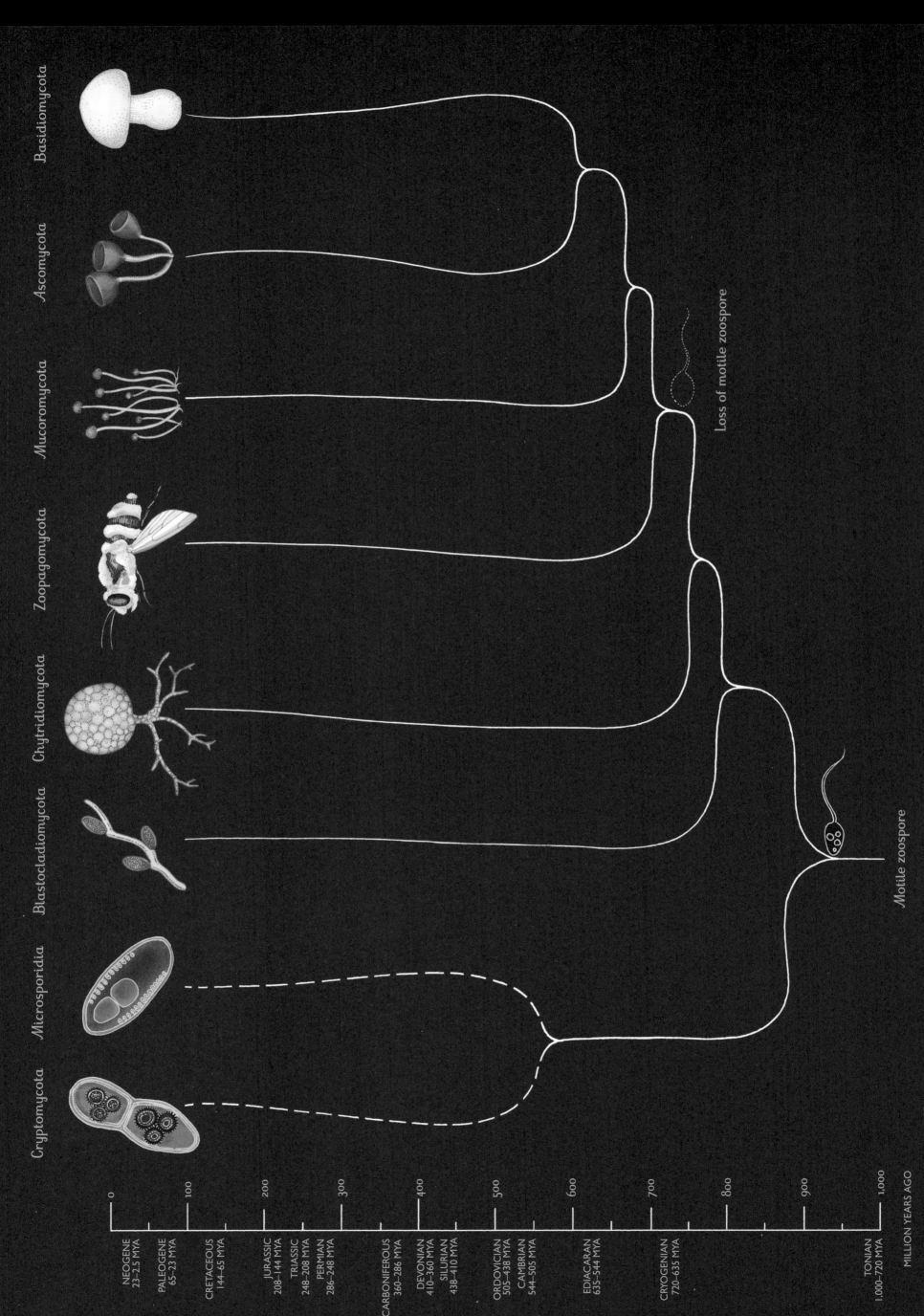

Cryptomycota   Microsporidia   Blastocladiomycota   Chytridiomycota   Zoopagomycota   Mucoromycota   Ascomycota   Basidiomycota

Loss of motile zoospore

Motile zoospore

0
100
200
300
400
500
600
700
800
900
1,000

NEOGENE
23–2.5 MYA

PALEOGENE
65–23 MYA

CRETACEOUS
144–65 MYA

JURASSIC
208–144 MYA

TRIASSIC
248–208 MYA

PERMIAN
286–248 MYA

CARBONIFEROUS
360–286 MYA

DEVONIAN
410–360 MYA

SILURIAN
438–410 MYA

ORDOVICIAN
505–438 MYA

CAMBRIAN
544–505 MYA

EDIACARAN
635–544 MYA

CRYOGENIAN
720–635 MYA

TONIAN
1,000–720 MYA

MILLION YEARS AGO

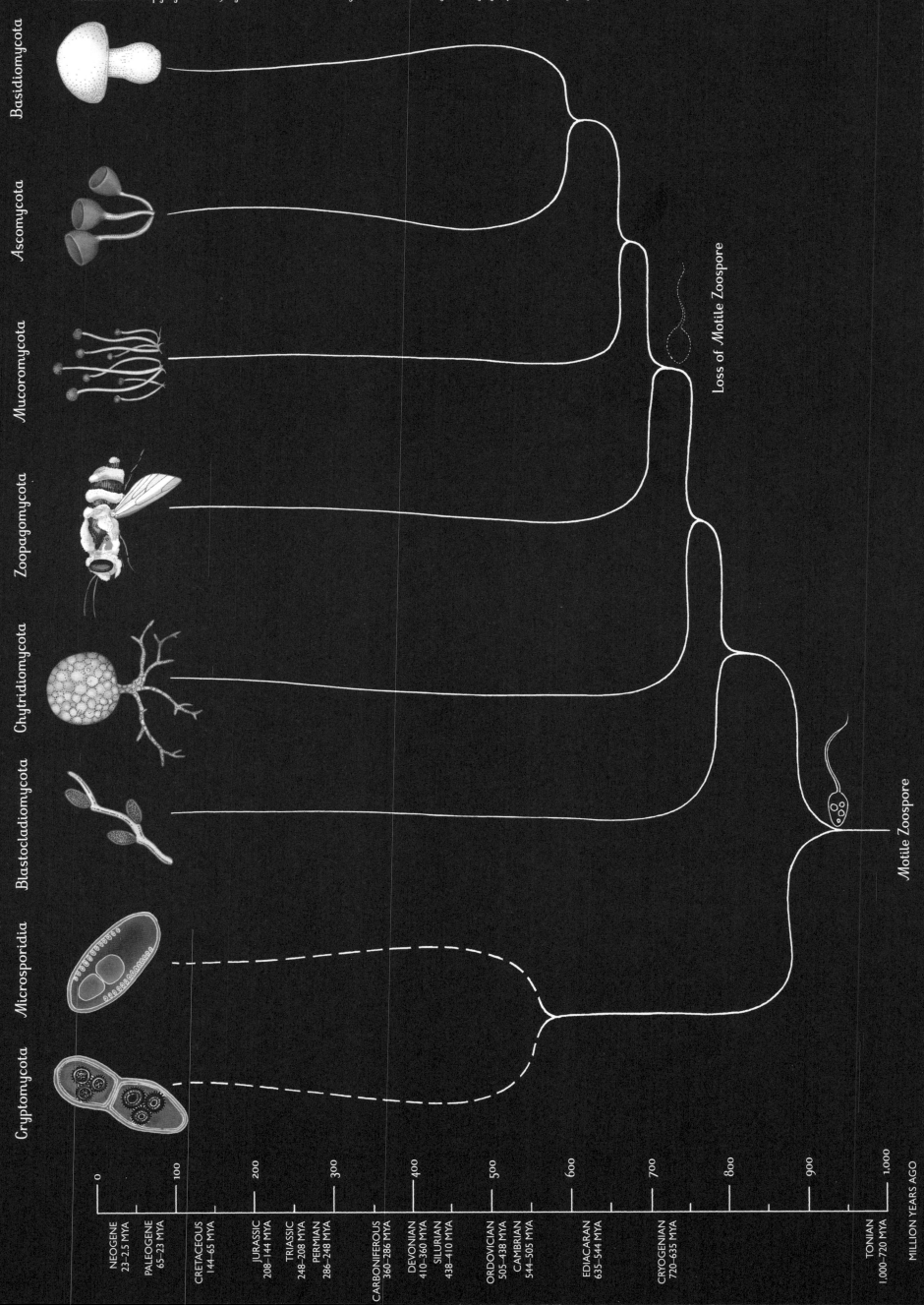